P9-CEJ-616

Garfield dishes it out

BY: JIM DAVIS

Ballantine Books • New York

Sale of this book without a front cover may be unauthorized.
If this book is coverless, it may have been reported to the
publisher as "unsold or destroyed" and neither the author nor
the publisher may have received payment for it.

© 1994 PAWS

All rights reserved under International and Pan-American Copyright
Conventions. Published in the United States by Ballantine Books, a
division of Random House, Inc., New York, and simultaneously in
Canada by Random House of Canada Limited, Toronto.

Originally published by Ballantine Books as three separate volumes.

Library of Congress Catalog Card Number: 94-96513

ISBN: 0-345-39287-6

Manufactured in the United States of America

First Edition: March 1995

10 9 8 7 6 5 4 3 2 1

GARFIELD'S TOP TEN COUNTRY PET TUNES

10. Daddy Sang Bass, Mama Had Worms

9. Lipstick on Your Flea Collar, Cheatin' on Your Mind

8. I Burp As Much In Texas As I Did I Tennessee

7. Call Me A Hairball Tomorrow, But Feed Me Tonight

6. Bubba Shot the Litterbox

5. Odie from Muskogee

4. Mamas Don't Let Your Kittens Grow Up To Be Professional Wrestlers

3. Walk Softly on This Tail Of Mine

2. You Used To Be My Chew Toy, But I Used To Have Some Teeth

1. Honky-Tonk Tabby (Gettin' Old... Feelin' Flabby)

MUNCH
MUNCH
MUNCH
MUNCH

© 1993 United Feature Syndicate, Inc.

JIM DAVIS 11-14

WHEW

BURP!

EXCUSE ME

© 1993 United Feature Syndicate, Inc.

© 1993 United Feature Syndicate, Inc.

YAWN

TODAY'S SUNDAY

SUNDAY IS THE DAY I ALWAYS PUT SOMETHING WEIRD IN JON'S FOOD

THIS RUBBER SNAKE SHOULD DO THE TRICK

JIM DAVIS 11-28

GARFIELD, THERE SEEMS TO BE A RUBBER SNAKE IN MY SALAD

© 1993 United Feature Syndicate, Inc.

IS TODAY SUNDAY?

BOY ARE WE IN A RUT

GARFIELD, YOU'RE FAT ENOUGH TO BE TWO CATS

JIM DAVIS 11-29

© 1993 United Feature Syndicate, Inc.

I'LL GO WITH THAT

FEED ME

SLASH!

© 1993 United Feature Syndicate, Inc.

THINKING OF YOU

JIM DAVIS 11-30

WHO ATE THE LASAGNA?

SOMETIMES I WORRY ABOUT YOU, JON

THAT WAS A RHETORICAL QUESTION

JON, I WANT YOU TO KNOW I'M TRYING TO CUT DOWN ON MY INSINCERITY

I THINK HE BOUGHT IT

© 1993 United Feature Syndicate, Inc.

I SUPPOSE WHEN YOU'RE THE FIRST SNOWFLAKE OF THE SEASON, YOU FEEL OBLIGATED TO MAKE A FLASHY ENTRANCE

GARFIELD, I KNOW YOU DON'T WANT TO GO TO THE FARM FOR CHRISTMAS, BUT WARM UP TO IT, OKAY?

HYUCK! HYUCK! HYUCK!

STOP THAT!

C'MON, GARFIELD! WE'RE LEAVING FOR THE FARM!

JUST A MINUTE...

HURRY UP!

WHAT WERE YOU DOING IN THERE?

LEAVING SANTA A FORWARDING ADDRESS

THERE'S SOMETHING SPECIAL ABOUT CHRISTMAS ON A FARM

SOMETHING UNIQUE, THAT YOU CAN'T GET ANYWHERE ELSE

SUCH AS CHRISTMAS COOKIES SHAPED LIKE FARM IMPLEMENTS

WE'RE VISITING JON'S FAMILY FOR CHRISTMAS

IT'S PEACEFUL HERE ON THE FARM

C'MON, GARFIELD! WE'RE GOING TO PLAY "TOUCH THE UDDER"

AND WEIRD

OKAY, YOU HOLD THAT STEADY, AND I'LL GO UP

WAIT A MINUTE!

WHY DO I ALWAYS HAVE TO HOLD THE LADDER? WHY DON'T **YOU** HOLD THE LADDER?!

BECAUSE I'M OLDER, THAT'S WHY!

© 1993 United Feature Syndicate, Inc.

OH, YEAH? WELL, I'M OLD ENOUGH TO GO UP NOW, TOO! MOVE OVER!

HEY! LOOKOUT! OW! STOPPIT!

WOOAAAHHH!!!

CRASH!

YOU BOYS STOP THAT FIGHTING AND GET IN HERE RIGHT NOW!!

WHAT AM I GOING TO DO WITH YOU TWO?

WHY DON'T YOU PLUG THEM IN?

JIM DAVIS 12-19

SNIFF SNIFF SNIFF SNIFF

CHRISTMAS IS IN THE AIR!

JIM DAVIS 12-20

© 1993 United Feature Syndicate, Inc.

AND HOT FROM THE OVEN!

COOKIES ARE READY!

HEY, DOC BOY, YOU LOOK LIKE A SISSY IN THOSE TEDDY BEAR PAJAMAS

JIM DAVIS 12-21

AT LEAST I DON'T LOOK LIKE A GEEK IN BUNNY PAJAMAS

© 1993 United Feature Syndicate, Inc.

BEARS! BEARS! BEARS!

BUNNIES! BUNNIES! BUNNIES!

TELL ME THEY WERE ADOPTED

I DON'T KNOW. I WAS OUT AT THE TIME

© 1993 United Feature Syndicate, Inc.

© 1993 Unitec Feature Syndicate, Inc.

SPLAT SPLAT
SPLAT
SPLAT
SPLAT
SPLAT
SPLAT
SPLAT
SPLAT

I'VE DECIDED AGAINST PURSUING A CAREER IN EGG JUGGLING

© 1993 United Feature Syndicate, Inc.

GARFIELD IS CHOOSING HIS WARDROBE FOR THE NEW YEAR'S PARTY

JIM DAVIS 12-30

NO, NO, THE POLKA DOTS JUST AREN'T YOU. TRY THE STRIPES

© 1993 United Feature Syndicate, Inc.

PERFECT

© 1994 United Feature Syndicate, Inc.

JIM DAVIS 1-9-94

PAT PAT PAT
PAT PAT
PAT

THIS IS A LITTLE WINTER TRADITION OF OURS

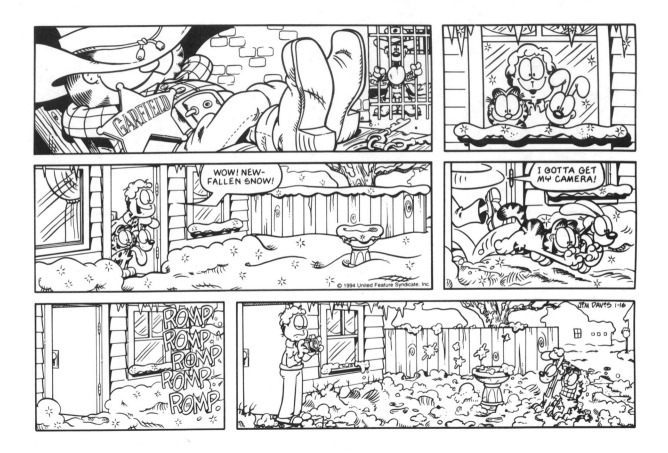

AH, YES. LIFE GOES ON

WHERE?

SIGH

SOME PEOPLE HAVE SOMETHING EXCITING AND NEW HAPPEN TO THEM EVERY SINGLE DAY!

SOUNDS MONOTONOUS

THEY SAY WATCHING TOO MUCH TV MAKES YOU PASSIVE

Jim Davis 1-31

NOT THAT I'M COMPLAINING

NOT THAT WE CARE

© 1994 United Feature Syndicate, Inc.

AND HERE'S TONIGHT'S EDITORIAL COMMENT

ARF ARF BOW-WOW BARK

Jim Davis 2-1

AND NOW, A REBUTTAL

© 1994 United Feature Syndicate, Inc.

MEOW MEOW PURRRR MEOW

THAT'S TELLING HIM!

THAT'S ENOUGH OF THAT

UH, I'M NOT THERE ANYMORE, ODIE

JIM DAVIS 2-9

YAWN

GARFIELD

GULP!

YAWN

I HAVEN'T SEEN HIS FACE IN TWO DAYS

GARFIELD

© 1994 United Feature Syndicate, Inc.

© 1994 United Feature Syndicate, Inc.

© 1994 United Feature Syndicate, Inc.

JIM DAVIS 2-20

I'VE BEEN DIETING

RIIIIIGHT

NO, REALLY. IS THIS A FACE THAT WOULD LIE?

HOW SHOULD I KNOW? I'VE NEVER SEEN IT

DIETING IS HARD WORK

BUT, AFTER SEVERAL GRUELING DAYS, I'M HAPPY TO REPORT I HAVE SLOWED MY WEIGHT GAIN TO A CRAWL!

A SMALL VICTORY PERHAPS, BUT A VICTORY NEVERTHELESS

YOU HAVE DOUGHNUTS ON YOUR BREATH

© 1994 United Feature Syndicate, Inc.

I WONDER WHAT IT'S LIKE OUTSIDE

IT'S RAINING

JIM DAVIS 3-2

© 1994 United Feature Syndicate, Inc.

AND BLOWING

I JUST BOUGHT COFFEE YESTERDAY, AND NOW WE'RE OUT

JIM DAVIS 3-3

DO YOU KNOW WHAT HAPPENED TO IT, GARFIELD?

COFFEE

© 1994 United Feature Syndicate, Inc.

NOT OFFHAND. BUT, IF YOU LIKE, I COULD STAY AWAKE FOR THE NEXT THREE NIGHTS TO GIVE IT MORE THOUGHT

COFFEE

© 1994 United Feature Syndicate, Inc

EVER NOTICE HOW CATS ARE ABLE TO BLEND INTO THE BACKGROUND?

JIM DAVIS 3-21

HERE'S A BALL OF YARN TO PLAY WITH

JIM DAVIS 3-22

© 1994 United Feature Syndicate, Inc

HOW DO YOU TURN IT ON?

CATS ARE CREATURES OF NATURE. WE DO THINGS BASED ENTIRELY ON...UH...

INSTINCT!

GARFIELD, IT'S DANGEROUS UP IN THAT TREE!

NOT FOR THE GRACEFUL CAT!

AT LEAST NOT FOR THE GRACEFUL CAT WITH A PARACHUTE

JON HURT HIS BACK AND CAN'T MOVE

3-30

© 1994 United Feature Syndicate, Inc.

I COULD GET HELP

OR I COULD GO THROUGH HIS POCKETS FOR CHANGE

GET AWAY FROM ME!

LADIES AND GENTLEMEN... ODIE!

© 1994 United Feature Syndicate, Inc.

THUD!

OPEN THE DOOR, **THEN** WALK IN!

JIM DAVIS 3-31

© 1994 United Feature Syndicate, Inc.

JiM DAViS 4-3

PENCIL

CHANGE

COMB

CORN CHIPS

FORK   MUNCH MUNCH MUNCH

AH-HA!

POP   THE REMOTE CONTROL

CLOMP CLOMP CLOMP CLOMP

JIM DAVIS 4-18

CLOMP CLOMP CLOMP

© 1994 United Feature Syndicate, Inc.

BEEN STOMPING SPIDERS?

HOW 'JA GUESS?

NO! NO! JON! DON'T DO IT!

© 1994 United Feature Syndicate, Inc.

JIM DAVIS 4-19

STOMP!

OH NO!!

I WANTED TO DO THAT

GOOD MORNING, GARFIELD

OH, ALL RIGHT. GOOD MORNING TO YOU TOO, POOKY

KISS

LOVE ME, LOVE MY TEDDY BEAR

JIM DAVIS 4-25

NOW DON'T KICK ODIE OFF THE TABLE!

ALL RIGHT, ALL RIGHT

BOOT!

THUD!

JIM DAVIS 4-26

© 1994 United Feature Syndicate, Inc.

JON SAYS I'M NOT CHEERFUL ENOUGH

JIM DAVIS 4-29

IS THIS CHEERFUL ENOUGH FOR YOU, BONE BRAIN?

© 1994 United Feature Syndica e, Inc

GET READY FOR A FANCY GOURMET MEAL, GARFIELD

© 1994 United Feature Syndicate, Inc.

VOILÀ!

A HOT DOG DRESSED IN A LITTLE TUXEDO?

JIM DAVIS 4-30

HEY, GARFIELD, WATCH ME IMPRESS THE CHICKS WITH MY MIME ACT

YOU LOOK LIKE A KITCHEN MATCH

JIM DAVIS 5-1

OW

AH, AH, AAAH... YOU'RE NOT SUPPOSED TO TALK

© 1994 United Feature Syndicate, Inc

JON'S OUT FROLICKING WITH MOTHER NATURE

RABID MOTH!

I WARNED HIM... THE WOMAN'S A MANIAC

FEELING DULL? WANT TO SEEM MORE EXCITING?

HANG OUT WITH SOMEONE EVEN DULLER!

WHAT IS IT, GARFIELD?

HE'S NEVER HAPPIER THAN WHEN HE'S WEARING HIS MUSICAL SOCKS

JON AND I HAD A LITTLE DISAGREEMENT THIS MORNING

BUT I HANDLED IT IN A MATURE MANNER...

YOU BROKE MY CRAYONS!

CONSIDERING WHAT I HAD TO WORK WITH

Garfield

CHEEERIP
CHEEERIP

NIGHT SOUNDS DON'T HAVE TO BE SCARY. FOR INSTANCE, THAT'S THE SOUND OF A CRICKET...

CHEEERIP
CHEEERIP

THAT'S THE HOUSE SETTLING

CREEEEK

PANT
PANT
PANT

...THAT IS ODIE

...THAT IS THE FAUCET DRIPPING

BLOOP
BLOOP
BLOOP
BLOOP

AND THOSE...

ARE JON'S GLOW-IN-THE-DARK BOXER SHORTS

© 1994 United Feature Syndicate, Inc.

© 1994 United Feature Syndicate, Inc.

garfield

WHAM!

PHHHHT!

© 1994 United Feature Syndicate, Inc.

JPM DAVPS 5-15

LOOK AT THAT CAT

TOO BAD OLD BOWSER ISN'T HERE

HE WAS A GOOD DOG

OLD BOWSER WOULD HAVE MADE AN ORANGE HAT OUT OF HIM

OLD BOWSER WOULD HAVE MADE A CAT TACO WITH HIM

YEP, TOO BAD OLD BOWSER ISN'T HERE

HE WAS A GOOD DOG

I HOPE THEY BURIED HIM DEEP

© 1994 United Feature Syndicate, Inc.

YOU SHOULD EXERCISE, GARFIELD

I'M ALREADY SO TIRED, IT DOESN'T SEEM NECESSARY

© 1994 PAWS, INC./Distributed by Universal Press Syndicate

JIM DAVIS 5-30

© 1994 PAWS, INC./Distributed by Universal Press Syndicate

ANY CHANCE YOU MIGHT ACTUALLY MOVE TODAY?

AN EARTHQUAKE IS ALWAYS A POSSIBILITY

JIM DAVIS 5-31

© 1994 PAWS, INC./Distributed by Universal Press Syndicate   JIM DAVIS 6·3

© 1994 PAWS, INC./Distributed by Universal Press Syndicate   JIM DAVIS 6·4

GARFIELD'S PARALLEL UNIVERSE

NIGHT IS DAY
AND BLACK IS WHITE...
BEHOLD A WORLD
OF INVERTED SIGHT!

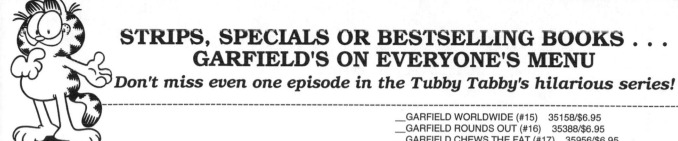

STRIPS, SPECIALS OR BESTSELLING BOOKS . . .
GARFIELD'S ON EVERYONE'S MENU
Don't miss even one episode in the Tubby Tabby's hilarious series!

__GARFIELD AT LARGE (#1)   32013/$6.95
__GARFIELD GAINS WEIGHT (#2)   32008/$6.95
__GARFIELD BIGGER THAN LIFE (#3)   32007/$6.95
__GARFIELD WEIGHS IN (#4)   32010/$6.95
__GARFIELD TAKES THE CAKE (#5)   32009/$6.95
__GARFIELD EATS HIS HEART OUT (#6)   32018/$6.95
__GARFIELD SITS AROUND THE HOUSE (#7)   32011/$6.95
__GARFIELD TIPS THE SCALES (#8)   33580/$6.95
__GARFIELD LOSES HIS FEET (#9)   31805/$6.95
__GARFIELD MAKES IT BIG (#10)   31928/$6.95
__GARFIELD ROLLS ON (#11)   32634/$6.95
__GARFIELD OUT TO LUNCH (#12)   33118/$6.95
__GARFIELD FOOD FOR THOUGHT (#13)   34129/$6.95
__GARFIELD SWALLOWS HIS PRIDE (#14)   34725/$6.95

__GARFIELD WORLDWIDE (#15)   35158/$6.95
__GARFIELD ROUNDS OUT (#16)   35388/$6.95
__GARFIELD CHEWS THE FAT (#17)   35956/$6.95
__GARFIELD GOES TO WAIST (#18)   36430/$6.95
__GARFIELD HANGS OUT (#19)   36835/$6.95
__GARFIELD TAKES UP SPACE (#20)   37029/$6.95
__GARFIELD SAYS A MOUTHFUL (#21)   37368/$6.95
__GARFIELD BY THE POUND (#22)   37579/$6.95
__GARFIELD KEEPS HIS CHINS UP (#23)   37959/$6.95
__GARFIELD TAKES HIS LICKS (#24)   38170/$6.95
__GARFIELD HITS THE BIG TIME (#25)   38332/$6.95
__GARFIELD PULLS HIS WEIGHT (#26)   38666/$6.95
__GARFIELD DISHES IT OUT (#27)   39287/$6.95

GARFIELD AT HIS SUNDAY BEST!
__GARFIELD TREASURY   32106/$11.95
__THE SECOND GARFIELD TREASURY   33276/$10.95
__THE THIRD GARFIELD TREASURY   32635/$11.00
__THE FOURTH GARFIELD TREASURY   34726/$10.95
__THE FIFTH GARFIELD TREASURY   36268/$12.00
__THE SIXTH GARFIELD TREASURY   37367/$10.95
__THE SEVENTH GARFIELD TREASURY   38427/$10.95

Please send me the BALLANTINE BOOKS I have checked above. I am enclosing $_____. (Please add $2.00 for the first book and $.50 for each additional book for postage and handling and include the appropriate state sales tax.) Send check or money order (no cash or C.O.D.'s) to Ballantine Mall Sales Dept. TA, 400 Hahn Road, Westminster, MD 21157.

To order by phone, call 1-800-733-3000 and use your major credit card.

Prices and numbers are subject to change without notice. Valid in the U.S. only. All orders are subject to availability.

Name_____

Address_____

City_____ State_____ Zip_____

Allow at least 4 weeks for delivery

BIRTHDAYS, HOLIDAYS, OR ANY DAY . . .

Keep GARFIELD on your calendar all year 'round!

GARFIELD TV SPECIALS
__BABES & BULLETS   36339/$5.95
__GARFIELD GOES HOLLYWOOD   34580/$6.95
__GARFIELD'S HALLOWEEN ADVENTURE   33045/$6.95
  (formerly GARFIELD IN DISGUISE)
__GARFIELD'S FELINE FANTASY   36902/$6.95
__GARFIELD IN PARADISE   33796/$6.95
__GARFIELD IN THE ROUGH   32242/$6.95
__GARFIELD ON THE TOWN   31542/$6.95
__GARFIELD'S THANKSGIVING   35650/$6.95
__HERE COMES GARFIELD   32021/$6.95
__GARFIELD GETS A LIFE   37375/$6.95
__A GARFIELD CHRISTMAS   35368/$5.95

Please send me the BALLANTINE BOOKS I have checked above. I am enclosing $_____. (Please add $2.00 for the first book and $.50 for each additional book for postage and handling and include the appropriate state sales tax.) Send check or money order (no cash or C.O.D.'s) to Ballantine Mail Sales Dept. TA, 400 Hahn Road, Westminster, MD 21157.

To order by phone, call 1-800-733-3000 and use your major credit card.

Prices and numbers are subject to change without notice. Valid in the U.S. only. All orders are subject to availability.

GREETINGS FROM GARFIELD!
GARFIELD POSTCARD BOOKS FOR ALL OCCASIONS.
__GARFIELD THINKING OF YOU   36516/$6.95
__GARFIELD WORDS TO LIVE BY   36679/$6.95
__GARFIELD BIRTHDAY GREETINGS   36771/$7.95
__GARFIELD BE MY VALENTINE   37121/$7.95
__GARFIELD SEASON'S GREETINGS   37435/$8.95
__GARFIELD VACATION GREETINGS   37774/$10.00
__GARFIELD'S THANK YOU POSTCARD BOOK   37893/$10.00
ALSO FROM GARFIELD:
__GARFIELD: HIS NINE LIVES   32061/$9.95
__THE GARFIELD BOOK OF CAT NAMES   35082/$5.95
__THE GARFIELD TRIVIA BOOK   33771/$6.95
__THE UNABRIDGED UNCENSORED
  UNBELIEVABLE GARFIELD   33772/$5.95
__GARFIELD: THE ME BOOK   36545/$7.95
__GARFIELD'S JUDGMENT DAY   36755/$6.95
__THE TRUTH ABOUT CATS   37226/$6.95

Name_____

Address_____

City_____ State_____ Zip_____
30   Allow at least 4 weeks for delivery   7/93 TA-267